Michael Stevens ᵥ
confusion and misinformation associated ......
rendous lifestyle. May this book serve to empower and
redirect those who need it most.

—DERRICK W. HUTCHINS, CHAIRMAN
GENERAL COUNCIL OF PASTORS AND ELDERS
CHURCH OF GOD IN CHRIST

I have known and respected Michael Stevens for many
years. He is both morally and intellectually qualified
to address issues related to the black family and sexual
behavior. I know that this book will bless all who read it.

—BISHOP CHARLES E. BLAKE, SENIOR PASTOR
WEST ANGELES CHURCH OF GOD IN CHRIST

THE CHURCH'S OFFICIAL

RESPONSE TO THE

EPIDEMIC OF

DOWNLOW LIVING

STRAIGHT UP

MICHAEL STEVENS

CREATION HOUSE
HOUSE
A STRANG COMPANY

Sis: Dominique!

May the

Lord Bless you!! prosper your life!

[signature]

STRAIGHT UP by Michael Stevens
Published by Creation House
A Strang Company
600 Rinehart Road
Lake Mary, Florida 32746
www.creationhouse.com

Unless otherwise noted, all Scripture quotations are from the New King James Version of the Bible. Copyright © 1979, 1980, 1982 by Thomas Nelson, Inc., publishers. Used by permission.

Scripture quotations marked NIV are from the Holy Bible, New International Version. Copyright © 1973, 1978, 1984, International Bible Society. Used by permission.

Scripture quotations marked KJV are from the King James Version of the Bible.

The names from the testimonials in Chapter 4 have been changed to preserve anonymity.

Cover design by Rachel Campbell
Interior design by David Bilby

Library of Congress Control Number: 2006926080
International Standard Book Number: 1-59979-013-0

First Edition

06 07 08 09 10 — 9 8 7 6 5 4 3 2 1

Printed in the United States of America

Acknowledgements

When I think of the many people who have patiently yet profoundly impacted my life and ministry, I humbly pause and ponder. Thank You, Jehovah-Jireh, for the continued provision of time, talents, and treasures. Thank You for the Paraclete (the Holy Spirit.) And thank You for Your most precious and sacrificial gift—Jesus, the Savior of the world.

Many, many thanks to my wife for life, Sharon, and my three children—Michael, Matthew, and little Charisma—for your uncomplaining patience and confidence in me. To my father, the greatest man I have ever known and followed. To my mother, for your many years of sacrifice and surrendering that I might have a chance to achieve. To my greatest unsung hero, my sister LaToya.

To my pastor and father in the Gospel, Apostle Otis T. Lockett. Thank you for being the greatest leader and example a man could ever have. To my encouraging and most incomparable warring angel, Pastor Patrick Wooden, thank you dearly for prophetically seeing and addressing this epidemic many years ago. To my many ministry mentors and friends, Bishop C. E. Blake, Bishop Vaughn McLaughlin, Bishop George Bloomer, Bishop Donald Hilliard, Bishop Brian Keith Williams, Chairman Derrick Hutchins, Pastor John P. Kee, thank you all for much motivation. To the entire University City Church family, especially the office staff, much, much appreciation. To all of the mighty, masculine, and straight men of God—stay the course; make the difference, for your wives and children are depending on you. Finally, to all of the recovering men who once were on the downlow and left to die, have courage, stay the course, and finish the race.

> Now unto Him who is able to keep you from falling, and present you faultless.
>
> —JUDE 1:24, KJV

Contents

Foreword . . . . *viii*

Introduction . . . . *x*

1 Seriousness of the hour 1

2 Homosexuals in denial:
uncovering the lies, deceptions,
and myths of down-low living 8

3 Advice from the down low is useless 14

4 Encourage, equip, and edify:
the very possibility of change 22

5 What the church must do right now 29

6 A little something for the "sistas" 39

Conclusion. 43

Notes. 45

Foreword

In this day of moral and spiritual relativism, Pastor Michael Stevens does a tremendous job of pointing out that the first casualty in the culture war is truth. These so-called, "down-low" brothers lie about the fact that they are bisexual, or as I put it "homosexuals practicing" (on women). They want to circumvent the word *bisexual* and pretend that the word does not apply to them, but bisexuals (men who have sex with women and men) are homosexuals.

We live in a day when it is popular to use euphemisms—words that make sin sound good. We live in a day of political correctness where the naked truth is not wanted or welcomed. The apostle Paul spoke of a day when men would not endure sound doctrine, but would seek out preachers who would tell them what they wanted to hear. (See 2 Timothy 4:3.) The prophet Isaiah said it this way:

> That this is a rebellious people, lying children, children who will not hear the law of the LORD; who say to the seers, "Do not see," and to the prophets, "Do not prophesy to us right things; speak to us smooth things, prophesy deceits."
>
> —ISAIAH 30:9–10

The prophet Jeremiah was told to "speak not in the name of the Lord" or he would be killed (Jer. 11:21). As it was in the days of Isaiah and Jeremiah, so it is today. There is a price to be paid for telling the truth. Praise the Lord that Pastor Stevens is willing to take up his cross and speak the truth.

The indifference of preachers has played a pivotal role

in the perversion invasion of the church in general, and the black church in particular. The silence is deafening! *Straight Up* deals with this silence. The truth must be proclaimed from the pulpits. As ambassadors for Christ we speak the truth in love—but we must actually speak that truth!

Straight Up is not a book that refuses to take a position. *Straight Up* takes the position that the Bible is right. *Straight Up* points out the fact that there is no such thing as a "straight" man who just so happens to have sex with other men. *Straight Up* declares in no uncertain terms the message of hope and deliverance. Read this book, digest it, and then spread the word about it. It proclaims the truth!

Pastor Stevens is gifted and called of God to bring this message to the body of Christ. I have preached at his church many times, and I must say the congregation bespeaks the message he conveys in this book. Having an ally like Pastor Stevens is a blessing indeed. He is a young man who is not afraid to take a position in a straightforward style that is easy to understand.

In our attempt not to offend anyone and in the name of love, we are allowing Satan to destroy our men, women, and children unopposed. Under the worldly definition of love, which the church has adopted, there is no correction, no judgment or rebuke, only "tolerance." Pastor Stevens understands that true love corrects, reproves, rebukes, and even makes judgment. *Straight Up* shines a love light on Satan's sinister plan to destroy the children of the God of the Bible. You will be both blessed and challenged as you read. This book is truly straight up!

—PATRICK L. WOODEN SR., DISTRICT SUPERINTENDENT
CHURCH OF GOD IN CHRIST

Introduction

There is a young man in the community who is sexually involved with another man; however, he does not consider himself to be gay. He is not feminine in appearance. In fact he is quite masculine and despite what others might say, according to him he is no homosexual. He is married with two children and is a deacon in his church, yet he is still drawn by his own lust not for another woman but for another man. He is no bisexual, either. So who or what is he? How should he be viewed? He is too manly to be titled "gay." He is too embarrassed and ashamed to be called homosexual. What he wants you and me to acknowledge is that he is...*on the downlow.* Does the church have any answers, any solutions for him? Like the Good Samaritan of old, does the church have any anointing oil for this man who is hurting and near death?

> Then Jesus answered and said: "A certain man went down from Jerusalem to Jericho, and fell among thieves, who stripped him of his clothing, wounded him, and departed, leaving him half dead. Now by chance a certain priest came down that road. And when he saw him, he passed by on the other side. Likewise a Levite, when he arrived at the place, came and looked, and passed by on the other side. But a certain Samaritan, as he journeyed, came where he was. And when he saw him, he had compassion. So he went to him and bandaged his wounds, pouring on oil and wine.
>
> —LUKE 10:30–34

WHY *STRAIGHT UP?*

The following passage is an excerpt from the book *On the Down Low* by J. L. King. Does the church have any anointing oil for him? Instead of ostracizing and unjustly condemning him, does the church have the anointing to pull him from the sin of homosexuality?

> I spotted this brother from my pew ten rows back. His broad shoulders seemed to take up two seats. His physique was not burly, but the definition of his muscles was noticeable even through his light wool suit. . . .
>
> [His wife] was pretty, too—a petite woman with a caramel complexion and straight hair, which she wore on this particular Sunday up in a conservative bun. He "Amen'd" every time the pastor hit his mark. I was new to this church. I made it my business to introduce myself to him after the service. When our eyes locked, I knew. He looked at me just a little too long. Mike worked for a mental-health organization in the Midwest and was a member of a Greek fraternity, a deacon in his church, and well liked. We hit it off instantly. He and his wife, who was six weeks pregnant, would hang out with my lady friend and me. His wife loved me and never suspected what either of us was up to. In her mind, if Mike was with me, he was cool because I was cool.[1]

The objective of *Straight Up* is to explain the seriousness and consequences of the wrongdoing of men who sleep with other men but consider themselves heterosexual. *Straight Up* will expose the many deceptions and snares of the down-low living phenomenon. *Straight Up* will explore biblical solutions for the healing and deliverance of men who have been greatly mislead. *Straight Up* is a practical insight relevant to today's issues in the black community; a biblical scholarship needed for salvation and success. *Straight Up* will serve as a teaching guide to pastors, church leaders, counselors, parents, and the soon-to-be patient brides of men who are destined to leave their sin behind and rise up to claim their God-given promises. Finally, *Straight Up* is an authoritative book representing the views of the church and particularly the strong, assertive, masculine, straight male clergy majority.

As you will soon find, one of the more subtle deceptions from the down-low camp is its deliberate confusing of the terms of that lifestyle. In response, I feel it is extremely important to stop the confusion from misnomers and mistitling. Let's clearly and comprehensively define right now what down-low living is: for the rest of this book I will interchangeably refer to down low, gay, bisexual, the homosexual agenda, "MSM" (men who sleep with men), and all the rest as homosexual, the homosexual lifestyle, and the down-low community.

This book is prayerfully written out of compassion and mercy for the many men of God whose lives have been blindly derailed and misaligned. This book is written out of severe and strict conviction, not callous and cold condemnation. For "God did not send His Son into the world to condemn the world, but that the world through Him might be saved" (John 3:17).

Almost on a daily basis now, I either read in the newspaper, view on a popular TV show, or hear talk around the city of another African-American man deciding to come out of the closet of shame and scorn, boasting with unsure confidence, his dual role of being a normal, straight family man who just happens to be attracted and sexually involved with other men. Even more disappointing is the expectation of acceptance these once-closeted homosexuals have for their lifestyle, which is not of the biblical will of God, nor of the design God has for man—a lifestyle of fruitfulness, faithfulness, and fidelity.

The down-low man is a man left half dead. At some point in his young life, he was violated—violently robbed and left bleeding, almost to the point of death on a roadside. He is expecting certain experts and counselors to help, but to no avail. They have ignored him completely, and honestly I do not care to help him either. I really don't. My mind tells me he probably deserved everything that has happened to him, and I don't care to help at all. After all, that is not, nor has it ever been, my struggle or sin. I really don't care to help this mostly dead man. Even as a pastor I think, *Let him die*—but I can't. There is a unique balance God has given me between the oil of anointing and the wine of care and concern.

As you can tell, I am upset—bitterly upset! Upset with a righteous indignation and kingdom mandate that wants to bring change that heals and makes whole—a change to the men, a change to the church, and a change to the community at large. This is precisely why I wrote *Straight Up*!

Right Now—In the Church

There has never been a more devastating time for the African-American family than now, facing this cancerous deterioration of its very fabric. As if this was not enough, it is also dealing with another chronic problem: it is now widely accepted that the majority of African-American households are headed by a single female parent. With more African-American men in penal institutions than all major colleges and universities, this new demonic destruction has been creeping in unseen. Equally perilous in this ongoing attack is the discrediting of the African-American church. The very place of hope and healing God has ordained and sanctioned will come to no avail if the covers of deception are not lifted and bridges of trust are not established.

I believe the answers of healing and deliverance are found in the church. The church must rise to the occasion and pour the anointing oil over those who are confused, bruised, and downtrodden. The African-American community must face the music and humbly realize that God has empowered the church to bring wholeness and healing as well as courage and confidence to change men who are struggling with down-low sin. "The local church is the hope of the world and its future rests primarily in the hands of its leaders."[2]

Growing up in the late seventies in a traditional African-American Baptist church, I saw my share of contradiction in the church. The most striking observation of my childhood also became the most hindering because it distracted me from committing to and serving the Lord as a young man—the flamboyant and feminine male role models in the church. From pulpits, choir stands, and usher boards, the normative acceptance of non-masculine men dominated the African-American church. It is sad to say, but in twenty-five years very little has changed. In fact, things seem to have gotten worse. Recently, a prominent African-American pastor known for reaching out to people with AIDS was caught making sexual advances toward another man. This same pastor had established transitional housing for people with AIDS and wanted to create awareness especially among African-American Baptist members who in the past had been resistant to "the gay white man's disease," as they commonly called it.[3] A couple of years later, according to local media, this pastor was caught sexually assaulting another man in his church office during a counseling session.[4] Audiotapes were released exposing the pastor's sexual promiscuities and a lawsuit was filed against him and the church.

Our churches are being badly represented compared to what God intended for His glory, not only behind pastors' desks, but also by gospel music television shows hosted by effeminate bishops and reverends. I wondered why so many soft, dainty men were drawn to the church. These were men who competitively wore broaches and blouses; men who screeched with high-pitched voices, wore a limp wrist, and walked real fast with chest elevated and pants a bit too tight—and then wondered why they were the target of crude jokes. Equally interesting was how many women of the church interacted with these womanly men with such naiveté while "doin' hair," shopping for clothes, talking about "the stories," and so on.

Can God deliver and set the captives free? Can the church facilitate God's healing and wholeness? Not according to J. L. King. In his latest book *Coming Up From the Down Low*, he says:

> I've been in small-town churches where pastors are running programs to "convert" men of questionable sexuality back to the literal straight and narrow and then marry them off—as if laying hands and praying will make a man who has sex with men into a heterosexual! This is crazy and just asking for trouble down the road. A person can call himself whatever he wants, but nature is going to find its way, and when it does, all hell will break loose.[5]

So, was Christ's life in vain? Was His death on the cross in vain? Was His precious blood for not? Certainly not! The apostle Paul reminds us in 2 Corinthians 6:1 to "not receive the grace of God in vain." I personally believe God can heal, deliver, and set my brothers totally free without returning to the sin lifestyle of homosexuality.

WHY ME?

So, your question now might be, "Who made you an authority of and for the church?" God has given me a unique and uncompromising sensitivity to the plight and disgust by the presence of feminine men in the church. As a young person, I had more diversity of church experience than most adults over a lifetime. During my first eighteen years I was actively involved in a Catholic church, an apostolic church, and a traditional Baptist church—all to which I was very observing and responsive. As a freshman in college I committed my life to the Lord. Afterward, I began serving as a minister in the Church of God in Christ. For the first time in my life in that particular church I actually saw real men—young, masculine men—who were serving the Lord. They were young men who had the vision and passion to make a difference in the church and in the community.

It was on the college campuses that I noticed the gospel choirs that counted among its members an overwhelming number of feminine men. At a neighboring college there was a high tolerance for the homosexual lifestyle among the students. It was there during a student evangelistic outreach that I realized a burden to minister to those young men who were trapped in a mindset of femininity. Today, my authoritative stand and apologetics are fueled by my work toward a master of divinity degree, and eventually a doctor of ministry. It is as a result of my academic endeavors that I am compelled to research and answer the questions of homosexuality, particularly within the African-American church.

My greatest asset in my authority and confidence speaking on behalf of the church is my passion for, and purpose of, being a man—all man. Just for the record, I have never at any time been a homosexual, been attracted to homosexuals, or ever considered the homosexual lifestyle. All of my needs are most satisfyingly fulfilled through the one woman of my life and marriage—my wife.

As I have traveled throughout this country and abroad, I have been very blessed to lead several men's conferences, retreats, seminars, and the like. When you visit the church I pastor, you see the number of young, masculine, African-American men who are saved, sanctified, and filled with the Holy Spirit. These men understand the importance of being the prophet, priest, provider, and protector of their homes. They also understand the importance of being the lover of one woman and a godly father to their children, whether they live in the same house with them or not. These are men of God who like others have their shortcomings, faults, and sins, yet they strive to be all that God has called them to be; all under the joy and satisfaction of being a manly man—a straight up man.

CHAPTER 1

Seriousness of the hour

The hour in which we live is grave. In our pop culture, from TV shows to movies, down-low terminology insidiously has crept into the mainstream of black America. First, there was R. Kelly's 2005 twelve-part *hip-hopera* song "Trapped in the Closet," in which a member of the clergy becomes the target of ridicule and scorn when it is revealed he is caught in a web of deception by his involvement with another man in a homosexual relationship. In the recent movie *On the Down Low*, two members of rival gangs from the south side of Chicago develop a homosexual relationship. Then there was *Brokeback Mountain*. Shamelessly set against the backdrop of the great American western, it showcases both homosexuality and adultery. Worse still, America is paying good money to see it. But TV and the movies do not hold a monopoly on this growing cancer. Just ask author Terry McMillan. She divorced the man who inspired her 1996 novel *How Stella Got Her Groove Back*, which recounted the romantic adventures of a forty-something woman who falls for a guy half her age. In papers filed in Contra Costa County Superior Court, McMillan said she decided to end her six-year marriage to Jonathan Plummer after learning he was a homosexual.[1]

"It was devastating to discover that a relationship I had publicized to the world as life-affirming and built on mutual love was actually based on deceit," McMillan said. "I was humili-

1

ated." In response, Plummer maintained McMillan treated him with "homophobic" scorn bordering on harassment since he came out to her as gay.[2] Does the church have any anointing oil for men such as this? Is there any healing balm for R. Kelly, Plummer, and McMillan, or for any couples living desperate lives of shame, brokenness, and pain?

THE IMPLICATIONS FOR BLACK AMERICA

Straight Up was originally conceived as a refutation of J. L. King's book *On the Down Low*. After reading his book, I became enraged and filled with righteous indignation. The book subtly misrepresents the sinful lifestyle, and in particular its overwhelming relationship to the black church. I believe his book serves as an ongoing recruitment device for homosexuals by listing popular places and Internet resources for men struggling and on the fence. After a deeper search of the subject matter, I realized this was bigger than him or his book. It was not about King's book nor his ex-wife Brenda Stone Browder's book, *On the Up and Up: A Survival Guide for Women Living with Men On the Down Low*. This situation is about a major epidemic in the African-American community. There were already major socioeconomic challenges facing the black man before the emergence of this destructive lifestyle—crime, unemployment, dysfunction, and illness among many others. Now we must deal with this invisible disease.

In King's latest book, *Coming Up From the Down Low*, he admits that many times his research or analysis work concluded in a desire to fulfill his lust for the men he was supposedly studying and helping:

> I was definitely learning things about these men's lives and was trying to keep it strictly informational, but, next thing you know, I was making quick hookups to satisfy my own lusts and desires. The conversations would take a sharp turn form interviews to seductions....I got caught

up and before I know it, I was deep back into a sexually risky and dishonest space—even though I kept lying to myself about the "research."[3]

The subject of down-low living has become a national phenomenon. From Oprah to *Ebony*, African-American men are becoming the freak show du jour. Downlowism has caught the attention of many so-called authorities. Welcome to the center ring, Mr. Keith Boykins and his book, *Beyond the Down Low*. At first glance, Boykins is a young, intelligent gentleman who seems to have solutions to this confusing lifestyle. This former Clinton White House aide gives an historical account of homosexuality and bisexuality within the African-American race. Though he mildly corrects J. L. King on several issues, Boykins is in denial about his homosexual life and is seeking to rationalize his confusing behavior. In fact, he even goes so far as to conclude that two of the greatest men of God in the Old Testament, Jonathan and David, were homosexual lovers. How desperate can this man be? Anyone with even a modest ability to interpret biblical doctrine would agree that the sentiments and affections Jonathan showed toward David were those of Christlike fellowship, support, and loyalty—not homosexuality!

> Then Jonathan said to David: "The Lord God of Israel is witness! When I have sounded out my father sometime tomorrow, or the third day, and indeed there is good toward David, and I do not send to you and tell you, may the Lord do so and much more to Jonathan. But if it pleases my father to do you evil, then I will report it to you and send you away, that you may go in safety. And the Lord be with you as He has been with my father. And you shall not only show me the kindness of the Lord while I still live, that I may not die; but you shall not cut off your kindness from my house forever, no, not when the Lord has cut off every one of the enemies of David

from the face of the earth." So Jonathan made a covenant with the house of David, saying, "Let the Lord require it at the hand of David's enemies." Now Jonathan again caused David to vow, because he loved him; for he loved him as he loved his own soul.

—1 SAMUEL 20:12–17

Yes, the hour is serious—very serious. There is a well-calculated plan to establish down-low living as acceptable in the black community. From the infiltration of coaches and mentors in little league sports to the presence of gay advertising, the homosexual agenda particularly against the black community is trying to bring a sense of inclusion and acceptance of the gay lifestyle that is destroying the foundation of the black family. Is this a "civil rights" issue? No way. African-Americans were born with the pigment of our skin color—there was no choice. Homosexuals, on the other hand, chose their sexual orientation. There is no such thing as being born with the so-called "gay gene."

In *Coming Up From the Down Low*, King gives his readers a startling revelation of sorts, "I'm a bisexual man. Making this statement is about as hard a thing as I've ever done....In my first book, *On the Down Low*, I described myself as a straight man who could find sexual gratifications with both men and women, but I also claimed that in my heart I could only find true love with a woman. I've come to this liberating truth: I'm not a straight man who has sex with men—I'm a bisexual man."[4] This is where I feel confusion and hurt have gotten the best of J. L. King.

Just recently, a study by psychologists at Northwestern University and the Center for Addiction and Mental Health in Toronto concluded that true bisexuality does not actually exist.[5] The study reported that there can be an attraction to either the opposite sex or the same sex, but not to both. What makes this study unique and defining is that it is the largest "non-self" study of its kind. People who claim bisexuality, according to the researchers, are usually homosexuals who are ambivalent about their homosexuality or are simply closeted. "Research on sexual orientation has been based almost entirely on self reports, and this is one of the few good studies using psychological measures," Dr. Lisa Diamond, Associate Professor of Psychology and Gender Identity at the University of Utah, said.[6]

The down-low community's primary strategic attack is against its largest opposition—the church. However, the church will not let her guard down; not today, not on my watch. While attempting to gain the empathy of and inclusion from the black community, the homosexual agenda seeks to assuage our conscience and obtain a level of tolerance for their sin and compromise. Their agenda is so strategically strong that it almost seems that these men are looking for sympathy from the black community for the choices they have made. These men must now be strongly considered "transporters" of death, not only to wife or girlfriend, but also to the very core of the black family. Because these men are willing to secretly lay with other men, only to follow that behavior with intercourse with their heterosexual wives, they are being referred to, as Linda Valleroy, a researcher at the Centers for Disease Control (CDC) in Atlanta, put it, as "bisexual bridges for HIV."[7] *Rolling Stone* magazine published an exposé on the growing population of homosexuals known as "bug-chasers."[8] These are homosexuals who purposely contract the AIDS virus. The article reported that many AIDS cases are made up of men who were actively seeking to be infected with the virus. These men are characterized by a bizarre, fatalistic obsession with death.

Since the Creation, there has always been an attack against the male seed. In Genesis, Cain attacked and killed his brother Abel. (See Genesis 4.) Pharaoh made a decree to have all male children murdered (Exodus 1). Today a new, similar decree

5

threatens our African-American male children. In his book, *Quitting America*, author Randall Robinson depicts many of today's "man-boys" from a scene in which he was walking to a drugstore after a speaking engagement in Rochester, New York:

> I happen into their midst while looking for a drugstore. There are more than twenty of them, these man-boys, trudging in and out of the damaged little bus shelter, moving a few feet this way, then that, not going anywhere this sunny school-day afternoon. Not going anywhere, period. They are the children of long-sown seed; old, burned Civil War canisters packed with live grapeshot, marked "DANGEROUS IF NOT TREATED." They are slavery's harvest.[9]

These are the same young men, Robinson believes, that, because of the theft of their history and their legacy, today have no earthly sense of worth and values:

> How pointless it would be to tell them now at this late stage of his death that the ancient Ethiopians were Christians when Europeans were pagans in idolatrous worship of their old gods, Pan and Diana. How could he possibly, so long after his social malformation, benefit now upon learning of the ancient manuscripts in the library at Timbuktu...I do not know what to say to him because I know of no other example in the modern world where millions of people from a single racial group had been stripped of everything save respiratory function—mother, father, child, property, language, culture, religion, freedom, and dignity.[10]

Noted author and lecturer, Dr. Jawanza Kunjufu, reminded us in the early nineties of the challenges facing young, black males in his book *Countering the Conspiracy to Destroy Black Boys*.[11] It was this alleged conspiracy against black boys which

I believe fueled Kunjufu's passion to explore and explain the various reasons why black men did not go to church.

The African-American male seed has regressed over the past several years due to ignorance of their history, uncontrolled circumstances in everyday life, and their absence from church. As if the consequences on African-American men were not enough, it now seems that the women in our lives receive the short end of the stick. It is believed that African-American women represent nearly 70 percent of new HIV cases. African-American women have a 1-in-160 chance[12] of getting AIDS, whereas white women have a 1-in-3000 chance.[13] Whether it is a husband, father, or son, much of what our sisters have endured emotionally, physically, or even psychologically has been the result of the harsh and negligent treatment from the African-American male. Does the church have any anointing oil to offer?

Homosexuals in denial: uncovering the lies, deceptions, and myths of down-low living

According to a Centers for Disease Control study published in 2000, almost 25 percent of black, HIV-positive men who had sex with other men *consider themselves heterosexual.*[1] Down-low living is a compromising sin lifestyle. The book *On the Down Low* contains a subtle deception and tactical trick, manipulating men to feel comfortable and accepted with their homosexual lifestyles. The subtitle itself, *Lives of Straight Black Men* is a treacherous misnomer. The effect of this dangerous teaching is that it draws people into this lifestyle and it can become a tool of recruitment. Books such as this have been strategically placed in the hands of many men who are already frustrated in their relationships with women, while at the same time listening to the mass media declaring that every man has a feminine side that he ought to acknowledge and get in touch with. *On the Down Low* longs for the underground network of homosexuals to grow. One of the most disturbing accounts given by King was a story about two men, "Andrew" and "D" who connected through the Internet.[2] "Andrew" was a closet homosexual and "D" was a married man with homosexual tendencies. After a preliminary encounter, the two finally satisfy their sinful urges. The account of these two men was laden with information about access and advertisements. From web addresses to meetings at a public mall, networking is presented to the curious, struggling reader. Of all the scenarios described throughout *On the Down Low*, this scene sickened me most.

There is a subtle theme running throughout this book that purports to discourage this lifestyle, but in fact is encouraging its defiling behaviors. The fact that the aforementioned scene takes place in the pews of the church between two seemingly healthy, satisfied men causes one to wonder if there is any standard of commitment at all in the black male. I realize that J. L. King is a homosexual in denial about his manhood, but I believe he is also confused about the purpose for which God created him and the man God has called him to be.

The devil is trying to confuse and cloud the subject with terminology and titles hoping to force men to tire, become confused, and retreat to acceptance and false cover in down-low living. King is a self-proclaimed heterosexual who just happens to be attracted to other men. This is nonsense of the highest order! He is a homosexual who needs to be delivered from the spirits of deception and bondage. King states in his book, "I knew those feelings of wanting to be with another brother were not dead; they were just asleep. They were not gone but on vacation. They were simply locked away...and I allowed [a man] to unlock that door."[3]

Deception begets deception. When a person has given him or herself over to sin and deception, one of their first moves is to begin searching for resources such as books, tapes, or other materials that help justify and bring comfort to the sin in which they are involved. Anything that is said or written with a glaze of religious wording will suffice. Such is the case in King's book and his quoting from Neale Donald Walsh's book, *Conversations With God*. King attempts to reinforce his position by citing Walsh, "Because God has given us free will, He will not punish us for the decisions we make."[4] This is patently absurd and absolutely unbiblical. It is the very poison that gives hope to homosexuals in the church. What they do not realize is that God gave man the ability to choose for the purpose of choosing between right and wrong. It is not Him who destroys us, it is man and his decisions that ultimately bring death and destruction upon his life. This is why we must acknowledge and understand the Bible as the definitive, authoritative Word of God. It is the standard of right living by which we all can live. Every man who wants to be set free must understand that advice from those yet ensnared in the web of deceit and destruction cannot be effective and will not profit you.

I believe the biggest deception of all is not of the spouse, family, or community, but of these men themselves. When a person has been deceived by the lies of the devil, the father of all lies (John 8:44), he will eventually begin to believe his own propaganda no matter how irrational it sounds. In *On the Down Low*, King categorizes all men into these groups: downlow, gay, bisexual, "ID–MSM" (non-identified men who sleep with other men), and straight.[5] Note the overwhelming ambiguity and overlapping of the definitions of those first four terms. A few chapters later, King categorizes the five different types of down-low men: the mature brother, the thug brother, the professional brother, the "I have a wife/girlfriend" brother, and the "I'm just curious" brother. Of the five categories, it was interesting that very little was said about the "I have a wife/girlfriend" brother:

> The need to hide my double lifestyle was so powerful that it overshadowed any common sense I had. As a result, my life was cloaked in lies.[6]

Does the church yet have any oil left? Is there any balm in

Gilead for these poor souls? During my preparation for this book I discovered an overwhelming avoidance of research concerning homosexuality. Perhaps this explains the avoidance of the very term *homosexual* in the down-low community. The down-low crowd is plagued with myths such as the age-old nature-versus-nurture debate. Homosexuality advocacy groups claim homosexuality is natural and genetic. I believe homosexuality is neither natural nor genetic, but is in fact nurture-based. According to the authoritative plan of life—the Bible—people are born with a particular sexual orientation:

> And the Lord God formed man of the dust of the ground, and breathed into his nostrils the breath of life; and man became a living being....And the Lord God said, "It is not good that man should be alone; I will make him a helper comparable to him."....And the Lord God caused a deep sleep to fall on Adam, and he slept; and He took one of his ribs, and closed up the flesh in its place. Then the rib which the Lord God had taken from man He made into a woman, and He brought her to the man.
>
> —GENESIS 2:7, 18, 21–22

God created the male with a natural desire for the female and the female with a desire for the male. It was only when men left their God-given affections and desires for a woman for unnatural, vile passions that their uncleanliness began to bear its due penalty. The homosexual who considers himself downlow has allowed social conditions to frame his choice to live this particular lifestyle:

> Therefore God also gave them up to uncleanness, in the lusts of their hearts, to dishonor their bodies among themselves, who exchanged the truth of God for the lie, and worshiped and served the creature rather than the Creator, who is blessed forever. Amen. For this reason

God gave them up to vile passions. For even their women exchanged the natural use for what is against nature. Likewise also the men, leaving the natural use of the woman, burned in their lust for one another, men with men committing what is shameful, and receiving in themselves the penalty of their error which was due. And even as they did not like to retain God in their knowledge, God gave them over to a debased mind, to do those things which are not fitting; being filled with all unrighteousness, sexual immorality, wickedness, covetousness, maliciousness; full of envy, murder, strife, deceit, evil-mindedness; they are whisperers.

—ROMANS 1:24–29

"The 'genetic and unchangeable' theory has been actively promoted by gay activists and the popular media. Is homosexuality really an inborn and normal variant of human nature? No. There is no evidence that shows that homosexuality is simply 'genetic.' *And none of the research claims there is a "gay" gene.* Only the press and certain researchers do, when speaking in sound bites to the public"[7] (italics mine). In fact, leading experts in the fields of psychology and social behavior conclude the following about the erroneous myths about the "gay" gene:

- Many scientists share the view that sexual orientation is shaped for most people at an early age through complex interactions of biological, psychological, and social factors.[8]

- At this point, the most widely held opinion [on causation of homosexuality] is that multiple factors play a role.[9]

- I know of no one in the field who argues that homosexuality can be explained without reference to environmental factors.[10]

- What the majority of respected scientists now believe is that homosexuality is attributable to a combination of psychological, social, and biological factors.[11]

Recently, television talk show host Dr. Phil got it publicly wrong and was officially corrected by Joseph Nicolosi, PhD, president of the National Association for Research and Therapy of Homosexuality (NARTH). Responding to an online question-and-answer session about homosexuality as a learned behavior, Dr. Phil stated that homosexuality was not a learned behavior but an inherited sexual orientation. Dr. Phil went on to say, "You are wired that way. Certainly some people will experiment with a gay lifestyle, and a gay person might experiment with a heterosexual one," to which Dr. Nicolosi responded, "Dr. Phil says sexual orientation is 'inherited,' which would mean 'genetic.' Dr. Phil should study this issue more carefully. There is no respected researcher who would agree with Dr. Phil. First, the biological components researchers have been finding are not primarily 'genetic.' Second, no one in the field is discounting environment, that is, parental and social influences."[12]

CHAPTER 3

Advice from the down low is useless

For every lie, there is truth. For every deception and myth, there is hope and healing. *For every sin and shame, there is the anointing oil.* Within the calamity and confusion of the down-low camp, there is an unspoken desire for help and rescue. After all, what could possibly quench the desires for unnatural sexual satisfaction after you tried the only physical options there are? Where else is there to go for the man who witnesses many of his comrades dying of AIDS, homicide, and suicide which are highly prevalent among the homosexual community? Where else is there to go when your whole life has reached the bottom of the downward spiral of debauchery and you have lost your wife, children, and all that you have worked for? The problem is that counsel for freedom and deliverance offered by men within that lifestyle simply does not work. As an example, King, who considers himself free from down-low living, states in his book, "The media needs to show two strong black men in a committed relationship living together and being positive in their community."[1] Is this any way of offering help to men struggling with and wanting out of that lifestyle? Is this the same down-low lover who does not want to be labeled queer, yet has the very same acts in common with them? While King is suggesting possible solutions for getting out, his book could be misused as a way to join the club. Several times throughout his book, King informs his

14

interested and perhaps curious readers how to find down-low men in parks and clubs in major cities as well as which Web sites and chat rooms to visit on the Internet.

The problem is that there is too much obsession with self: self-awareness, self-esteem, self-preservation...Jesus said to deny yourself. (See Matthew 16:24.) Self has already proven unreliable and undependable. There is always an appetite for sin in this self, as King stated, "This need was not going away," and "He was willing to try and control it."[2]

Along with the spirit of deception and self-reliance comes the spirit of confusion. One theme taken from many of the reading materials on down-low life is the consistency of a commitment to confusion. Here is an example: "When athletes engage in homosexual behavior, it does not necessarily mean they are homosexual."[3] What on earth can this possibly mean? Either you are or you are not—if I steal, I am a thief; if I lie from time to time, I am a liar. When you are talking about the down-low homosexual life, everything that is, isn't, and everything that isn't, is—the whole thing is all one large exercise in smoke-and-mirrors! Self-described homosexual champion Keith Boykins suggests:

> If we truly hope to break the cycle of the down low, we have to create an environment where men can be free to be who they are, and not just who we expect them to be. Being a black man has nothing to do with your sexual orientation. It has everything to do with your sense of honesty, fairness, duty, and courage. And many of the greatest black men who personify that courage were gay or bisexual themselves.[4]

Boykins goes on to mention several men from various backgrounds including entertainment, sports, and even ministry, who were either gay or bisexual. I have never heard of most of them, with the exception of the Reverend James Cleveland.

Boykins suggests there is much to learn about manhood, particularly masculine manhood, from older homosexual men.[5] So, here's my question: how can a so-called man, who has shirked his God-given calling and giftings as a man for the lust of a male lover, tell me or any other straight man anything about manhood? I mean, there is absolutely nothing a middle-aged homosexual who has lost his personal battle of confusion and compromise with masculinity and manhood can tell me about being a man.

Even in a support-group environment—these groups of gay, feminine men who are attempting to solve life's problems and how they became who and what they are—this just will not work. In fact, those who counsel homosexuals suggest that one of the major drawbacks to many homosexual support groups is that everyone in the group is struggling with the same problem. "If you are in the same pit, who's going to pull you out? You've got to be in a healthy community, a healthy church, and risk being vulnerable to people who you think may not understand," says Jeff Buchanan of New Song Christian Fellowship in Brentwood, Tennessee.[6] It repeatedly has been proven that the successful approach in ministering to recovering homosexuals is the ongoing interaction with, and presence of, strong, masculine, straight men. "What the church has to realize is that in order for a person with homosexual tendencies to see freedom, they need to be with healthy men. They need to be with families. They need to be with grandmothers and grandfathers and children. They need to have that healthy family community aspect," says Buchanan.[7]

Yes, perhaps the church does have the anointing oil.

The Theological Perspective

One of the biggest myths maintained among the down-low camp is that homosexuality is not a sin and even if it was, Jesus never preached against the sin of homosexuality in the first place. This so-called gay theology is nothing more than a convenient twisting of Scripture. Pastor Tim Wilkins, a former homosexual, recently spoke to the Apologetics Association on the campus of the University of Wisconsin-Milwaukee. Pastor Wilkins told the audience, including attending homosexuals, "Change for the homosexual is less about flipping a switch and more about turning a knob." Concerning gay theology, Wilkins said, "Gay theology is a reinterpretation of Scripture to say what Scripture does not really say. It is a reinterpretation to find loopholes to justify actions and sin." He told the local homosexuals, "You can choose to abstain from...homosexual activity. Rest assured that with time and obedience, the attraction for [the same sex] will diminish and the attraction for [the opposite sex] will increase."[8]

In the summer of 2005 in the city of Charlotte, a couple of churches including ours decided to share the Gospel during the Black National Gay and Lesbian Weekend, the largest event of its kind in the South. Though I was prepared to minister to many men and women, I was not prepared to deal with the elders and pastor of the homosexual church in our area. In conversation after conversation, people agreed that murder, fornication, rape, and the like were all blatant, biblical sins, but when it came to the sin of homosexuality, there was no agreement. Our men confronted the sin of homosexuality while showing determined and compassionate love for those who were lost. What was not surprising was the overwhelming reception of many men who acknowledged their error and sin. The joy for me that day was to personally witness many men receiving salvation as well as confessing their wrongdoing. Many of the attendees of the homosexual rally admitted their need for salvation and deliverance. One young man I recall vividly just looked out of place. Not because he was masculine and thuggish looking, but because he spoke with an "I can't believe I'm really here in this queer environment," tone to his voice.

17

When I asked him why he was there, he responded that he was curious and had been invited by a friend. I asked him if he really wanted to be there, and he said no. After I encouraged this young brother to get to know the Father's will for his life, I charged him to break every association with the homosexual community and live his life for God. To God be the glory, many men that day were prayed for with many confessing their sins and some led to the Lord. My presence at that event was preceded by an editorial I wrote that was published in the *Charlotte Observer*.

THE SPIRIT OF SIN AND SYNCRETISM

The sin of homosexuality is an issue of syncretism. Jesus never mentioned the word *homosexual* in the Gospels, nor did He say anything about or preach against homosexual sin. However, Jesus also never mentioned terms such as *gang rape, Internet pornography,* or *pedophilia* that we acknowledge today as sin. Jesus preached clearly and emphatically against sin, to "go and sin no more" (John 8:11). Lust, adultery, fornication, and rape are sins just as much as homosexuality is.

One of the questions homosexuals like to debate is, "After God made Adam and Eve, who are we to say that God also didn't create a Steve for Adam?" The answer? God did create a Steve...not for Adam, but for Stephanie. How do you think procreation continued? The problem was that because sin entered the Garden, it entered the lives of all those that were living during the time of the Creation. The homosexual agenda would have us believe that Steve has now left Stephanie and has taken a liking to another man. It was not long after Creation when men refused to have sex with women only to violate the two visitors of Lot in Genesis 19:

> Before they had gone to bed, all the men from every part of the city of Sodom—both young and old—surrounded the house. They called to Lot, "Where are the men who

came to you tonight? Bring them out to us so that we can
have sex with them."

—GENESIS 19:4–5, NIV

This was the last we ever heard of Sodom and Gomorrah
before the judgment of God. The Book of Romans comprehensively describes how we got where we are today with the
homosexual, down-low lifestyle:

> For the wrath of God is revealed from heaven against
> all ungodliness and unrighteousness of men, who sup-
> press the truth in unrighteousness, because what may be
> known of God is manifest in them, for God has shown
> it to them. For since the creation of the world His invis-
> ible attributes are clearly seen, being understood by the
> things that are made, even His eternal power and God-
> head, so that they are without excuse.
>
> —ROMANS 1:18–20

For those who truly want out, the spirit of sin and syncretism must be boldly confronted. The word *syncretism* describes
the ability to mix right and wrong. When studying the trends
of down-low living, I find it interesting that these men cannot
only go to church, but also preach in the pulpit, sing in choirs,
usher at the doors, and serve on boards and committees. Many
of the homosexual authors writing on the subject of down low
often describe praise and worship, perseverance prayer and
fasting, and seeking God's will.

The most grating part of the researching and writing for
this book was reading through the down-low community's
constant mixing of God, His will, acceptance, and guidance
for their homosexual living. Many down-low men now claim
a divine "feeling" that they are called and compelled by God to
write on this issue. They speak of living "in the Resurrection
of God's love and are [now] at peace,"[9] yet they are in obvious

and, by their own admission, complete sin. Statements such as "God's purpose" and "prayers answered" are strategic target words homosexuals now use to infiltrate, contaminate, and attempt to fuse the two infusible extremes: God's perfect will and man's imperfect, compromising lifestyles.

King, like many other homosexual activists, feels that he is commissioned by God to go and spread the gospel of acceptance and norm. In *Coming Up From the Down Low*, King states, "I know what I have done is the right thing. I know that I have to learn to deal with the bitter as well as the sweet. But if I continue to allow God to use me, he will keep me protected and he will order my steps. For this year, my scriptural affirmation is: No weapon formed against me shall prosper."[10] What King does not realize is that Bible principles can only be operable for those who live the Bible, not just quote the Bible. Can the rapist, the murderer, or the child molester quote the same Scripture during their heinous crimes? (See John 8:44.)

Syncretism has allowed them to mix a little bit of holiness with a little bit of horse apples. Where sin and syncretism are invited into a life, pride and destruction follow near behind. Pride goes before destruction and a haughty spirit before a fall. (See Proverbs 16:18.) Such was the case with J. L. King. Isaiah 59:1–2 reminds us that it is not the Lord's hand that is slack, but our sins have separated us from God. When King, who was raised in a God-fearing home, was abiding in his role as a husband and father, the favor of God was upon him and was evident in his job, home, and income. There was an overwhelming parallel to his right standing and God's blessings. As King left the order and commandments of God, he began to slowly lose the very blessings and favor he had obtained. Malachi 2 warns the husband that is unfaithful toward the wife of his youth. God's blessings were upon those that honored their wives and adamantly judged those men who were unfaithful. "Righteousness exalts a nation [people], but sin is a reproach to any people" (Prov. 14:34).

20

In our church, I have been teaching our men for years that God has called them to be the priests of their homes. As the priest of our homes, we men have a responsibility to establish an everlasting presence of God in our homes through commitment and devotion. While the wife is the manager of the home, the man still has a divine position as the head of his home. One of the primary functions as priest of your home is to discern and recognize the demonic.

Spiritual warfare and the demonic are subject matters ministered upon very rarely in the church today. In fact, if we as pastors would personally engage ourselves again into fasting, prayer, and spending time before the face of God, an example would be set and carried out by the men of our church. Instead, we preach the gospel of meisms, egoisms, greed, and gain.

All the while, our ministers of music are eyeing brother after brother. Because the church choir stand has been for a long time the bedrock of artistic and emotional expression for the black church, I believe many of the homosexual overtones went unnoticed and ignored amidst the sensationalism of loud music, expressive shouting and dancing. This combined with the fact that many musicians and choir directors were tremendous influencers in the church, say nothing for their weekly contribution to successfully delivering a "high" emotional service that led to a "don't ask, don't tell" policy. Consequently, many pastors were caught in a catch-22 position between successful worship services and immoral behavior in the choir stand.

What happened to warfare? Why are we not reminded in the church today that the weapons of this war are not carnal? This fight against the homosexual agenda cannot be fought with flesh and blood or candlelight vigils, marches, political muscle, civil, or social means. The church does have anointing oil to offer.

CHAPTER 4

Encourage, equip, and edify: the very possibility of change

Is change possible for the struggling, down-low brother? I say and I know that it is very possible. Throughout my many years in ministry, I have been very fortunate to see the before-and-after scenario of men and women who allowed God to impact their lives and bring revival, renewal, and reform. A courageous group of men recently published an article concerning their personal change and deliverance from the pain and pressures of homosexuality:

> Homosexuality just wasn't right for us. It conflicted with our deeply held beliefs, our life goals, and our intrinsic sense of our true, authentic selves. And so we pursued change—and ultimately found that by facing and addressing deep emotional wounds, fears, and other root problems, our homosexual desires started to diminish and then to disappear, while heterosexual feelings began to emerge and increase. True, the journey was often difficult and frightening, but the destination has brought us immeasurable peace and joy. In fact, if there is one consistency in the scores of published testimonials by those who have succeeded at change, it is their universal claim that their lives are better now.[1]

Revelation 12:11 reminds us that they overcame him (the

devil) by the blood of the Lamb and by the word of their testi-
mony. The following are a few testimonies of men who at one
time were trapped in the grip of homosexuality, but by the
grace and power of God today are free:

> The journey has been the hardest thing I've ever done,
> but it was worth it. Today, I am a different man—stron-
> ger, healthier, happier, more loving, more confident, and
> more mature. I am a better father, a better husband, a
> better friend, and a more devoted son of God. I would
> never trade the peace, growth, and healing I have experi-
> enced for anything in the world.
>
> —Jamal

> I am at the point in my life now where homosexuality is
> no longer a struggle. I have had to get past a lot of obsta-
> cles—psychologically, spiritually, and emotionally—to
> get to the point of resisting temptation. I am very fulfilled
> in my life. I no longer want homosexuality in my life. I no
> longer need it. Today, I identify with other heterosexual
> men as my peers, my brothers, and my equals. I am in
> love with my wife. I love being a husband and a daddy.
>
> —Terrance

> I now feel I have successfully transitioned from gay and
> bisexual to straight. The change is immensely satisfying
> and rewarding. I started dating women again because I
> wanted a healthy relationship that would last. I will settle
> down with one, eventually. I am a stronger man now, bet-
> ter prepared to be in a close relationship, with more to
> give as a whole man.
>
> —Abdul

THE NEED FOR ANOINTING OIL:
COMPASSION AND COMMITMENT

So, what will work? What will effectively bring change to this epidemic? There must be the ever-so-delicate impartation of truth and grace. Ephesians 4:15 reminds us to "speak the truth in love." At the same time, it is and must be true grace that saves us. (See Ephesians 2:8.) Because God's grace is sufficient, those who are weak in their will to live holy can become whole through grace. This unique balance of grace and truth can only derive from the authority of the Bible. Here is a biblical passage that I use as the foundation for bringing healing and deliverance to the men of the down-low community:

> Then they came to the other side of the sea, to the country of the Gadarenes. And when He had come out of the boat, immediately there met Him out of the tombs a man with an unclean spirit, who had his dwelling among the tombs; and no one could bind him, not even with chains, because he had often been bound with shackles and chains. And the chains had been pulled apart by him, and the shackles broken in pieces; neither could anyone tame him. And always, night and day, he was in the mountains and in the tombs, crying out and cutting himself with stones. When he saw Jesus from afar, he ran and worshiped Him.

In this passage, the men needing ministry are near death. Like these men of old, men today living the down-low life are men who, as Scripture declares, are only a step away from death. These are men who are still living in the natural realm, yet their souls are in intensive care with very little time to recover. Thank God for Jesus: like the Samaritan who had the compassion of Christ on the inside, Jesus Himself takes notice of the desperate, crying man in the tombs. The man who was near death shares several interesting and true characteristics with men on the down low:

- Has been bound (Mark 5:4)
- Living among the dead (v. 2)
- Desires to come to Jesus and his glorious church (v. 2)
- Desires to worship God (v. 6)
- Crying out (v. 5)

Looking at this man in the tombs I realized that the motive of the down-low brother is not to defiantly impose his presence on the church. He has a true longing for freedom from the bondage of this sin. St. Augustine reminds us "inside every man is a 'God-shaped' void."[2]

In order for the church to minister effectively to our hurting and confused brothers, we must first realize the malpractice of their community. They have mistaken the sins and compromises of their lifestyle as a "mind only" problem and not a "soul" problem. There were four things Jesus did for the man in the tomb that we as clergy leaders can do to bring total healing and deliverance to struggling men today:

- Have the *courage* Jesus had to confront the issues of our families, churches, and community.
- Have the *compassion* Jesus had (Jude 20).
- Take *control* of the situation (Jude 9).
- *Command* deliverance and breakthrough with authority (Jude 13–15).

Out of these Scripture passages we can identify four principles for breakthrough and deliverance. These non-negotiable principles can be applied to the brother in your realm of influence that is seeking change.

The first is acceptance. If the struggling man is ever to have healing from God, to his own self he must be true. Acceptance is not justification or rationalization. It is the full acknowledgement of wrongdoing and error. It is the admitting of sin—missing the mark that God has established for the man's life. First John 1:9 states, "If we confess our sins, He is faithful and just to forgive us our sins and to cleanse us from all unrighteousness. If we say that we have not sinned, we make Him a liar, and His word is not in us." The patriarch David sinned much. Murder, deception, and adultery ridded his life, yet because of his unique ability to be truthful and transparent with God, he was repeatedly forgiven and delivered from his iniquities and transgressions:

> Have mercy upon me, O God, according to Your loving-kindness; according to the multitude of Your tender mercies, blot out my transgressions. Wash me thoroughly from my iniquity, and cleanse me from my sin. For I acknowledge my transgressions, and my sin is always before me. Against You, You only, have I sinned, and done this evil in Your sight—that You may be found just when You speak, and blameless when You judge. Behold, I was brought forth in iniquity, and in sin my mother conceived me. Behold, You desire truth in the inward parts, and in the hidden part You will make me to know wisdom. Purge me with hyssop, and I shall be clean; wash me, and I shall be whiter than snow. Make me to hear joy and gladness, that the bones You have broken may rejoice. Hide Your face from my sins, and blot out all my iniquities. Create in me a clean heart, O God, and renew a steadfast spirit within me. Do not cast me away from Your presence, and do not take Your Holy Spirit from me. Restore to me the joy of Your salvation, and uphold me by Your generous Spirit. Then I will teach transgressors Your ways, and sinners shall be converted to You. Deliver me from bloodshed, O God, The God of my salvation, and my tongue shall sing aloud of Your righteousness. O Lord, open my lips, and my mouth shall show forth Your praise. For You do not desire sacrifice, or else I would

give it; You do not delight in burnt offering. The sacrifices of God are a broken spirit, a broken and a contrite heart—these, O God, You will not despise.

—Psalm 51:1–17

Second, *transparency* must be carried to the next level of responsibility and accountability. Struggling men must be honest with other sound, solid, and secure men who have the spiritual maturity to discern deliverance and change. There is safety in the multitude of counselors. As embarrassing as the down-low lifestyle is, the brother must come forth and be willing to face what he wants fixed in his life. It will be at this time that true repentance can happen.

The word *repentance* has been thoroughly avoided and ignored. God is willing that no man would perish but have everlasting life. (See 2 Peter 3:9.) At best, we have created all sorts of alternatives and substitutes to what God is commanding for today. In times past God has winked at our ignorance, but now is commanding men everywhere to repent. (See Acts 17:30.) True repentance must be more than feeling sorry for the sins committed, or at best coming to the altar knowing that we have no will to turn or change. Repentance is not a 360-degree turn, but a 180-degree turn.

The word *repent* means to have a change of heart or mind. It means to come from the basement of lifestyles and return to the penthouse of God's original plan for your life. How important is repentance? It is the lifeline of those seeking salvation and surrendering, "unless you repent you will all likewise perish" (Luke 13:3).

Thirdly, avoidance from any person, place, or thing that might remind them of their past challenges to compromise must be achieved at all cost!. As the Scripture says, abstain from "every kind of evil" (1 Thess. 5:22). Old friends, lovers, and relationships must be cut off for the sake of having a second chance at life. Past chat rooms, lounges, and parks must never again be visited to fulfill fleshly desires. Probably the toughest of all is to cut off any conversations or communication with anyone fueling the fire of sin and compromise with the down-low lifestyle. "Be not deceived: evil communications corrupt good manners" (1 Cor. 15:33, KJV).

Finally, there has to be confidence. Not confidence in the flesh or in self-reliance, but confidence in God your Creator; confidence that one function of the Holy Spirit is to convict you of sin and keep you from falling back into sin. Confidence brings a certain level of security and success that no matter the insurmountable challenges ahead, a man can and will conquer them.

> Being confident of this very thing, that he which hath begun a good work in you will perform it until the day of Jesus Christ.
>
> —PHILIPPIANS 1:6

CHAPTER 5

What the church must do right now

There is no doubt in my mind that it is God's will that homosexuals be totally healed and delivered from their sin and compromise. We as pastors and church leaders must be as willing to see healing and breakthrough for our brothers as God is. For the leader of the church, it starts with the mind-set. Mind-sets of leaders must change toward ministering healing and deliverance to those who today are considered outcasts. I believe the local church is the hope of the world. God will hold the local church accountable for the lack of ministry and care our brothers need in these critical hours. Noted author and pastor Bishop Brian Keith Williams suggests in his book, *Ministering Graciously to the Gay and Lesbian Community*, that the reason the church shuns and harshly judges the homosexual, the cross-dresser, the transvestite, and the transsexual is that we have no oil of anointing for them, and consequently we put them in the back row of the sanctuary and eventually out of the church.[1]

But the church must act now. Yelling foul epithets from the pulpits of America's churches might be crowd moving and entertaining, but God still sees those people as lost souls for whom His Son's precious blood was shed. He still wants no man to perish, but have everlasting life.

29

THE PROCESS TOWARD WHOLENESS

The first step in healing for those who struggle with the down-low life is to bring restoration from the church. Zechariah 9:12 cries, "Return to the stronghold, you prisoners of hope. Even today I declare that I will restore double to you." When *On the Down Low* was written, the stage was set inside the black church for a direct attempt to discredit and attack the authority of God's power. In chapter 1, a scene of sin and compromise is established with an ungodly encounter between two homosexuals in denial. Where are they? In the pews! The church is the target of choice because homosexuals have found that no matter how low their sins, they cannot live without the inspiration and communal gathering of the black church. There is an attempt to gain acceptance from God's clergy leaders. The discrediting of the church is becoming more and more the norm in our country, with some examples more overt than others. Recently in *Ebony* magazine, I was alarmed to see the lack of respect shown to the contributions of the black church to the black community. While so many other venues were paraded for their impact and influence on black America, the church was recognized as if it was the proverbial ostrich with its head in the sand. Certainly, I suggested to them, the centerpiece of security and strategy throughout the civil rights movement is more influential than they gave it credit:

Dear *Ebony* Magazine:

I was extremely saddened and quite disheartened to observe the lack of prominent "ministry faces" in your recent sixtieth anniversary issue of *Ebony*. Where were the faces of religious black America? In particular, where were the male leaders of religious black America?

In comparison with the other areas of celebration in your magazine (movies, TV, politics, sports, and music), the religious venue mentioned only a few personalities and pictured one image while all other venues averaged count- less personalities and at least twelve pictures per venue. In the two and one-half page blurb you so graciously gave the church, 90 percent of the church leaders mentioned were women. I have nothing against women leaders in the church, but in such a critical time of absentee black male leadership, couldn't you have at least shown a couple of black male religious leaders? Again, where were the faces of black religious leaders?

In your article, you called the black church a "dominant presence and stabilizing force" in the African-American community. I agree. In the last sixty years the church has been the most consistent cornerstone of the black community particularly during the civil rights era when the church was the war room of prayer and strategic planning. The church was also the launching pad for such leaders as Dr. Martin Luther King Jr. and Reverend Jesse Jackson. As then, today the seat of empowerment and authority yet lies within the black church. Much social improvement and empowerment today are still propelled in and by the black church, which is led by some incredible black leaders.

Please help me not to think that this is a subtle attack to discredit the church of her influence, independence, and identity. Where was the respect, right appreciation, and reverence for the most anchored institution of our community in the last sixty years?

Concerned,

Pastor Michael A. Stevens Sr.

We often preach in the church, "So the shepherd, so the sheep." If the anointing flows from the head down, I believe the spirit of compromise does, too. One of the biggest challenges in bringing healing to the down-low community is the spirit of *downlowism* behind the sacred desk. It is sad to say, but this problem is the very spirit of denial we are trying to encourage men on the down low to overcome. There have been many accounts around the country of pastors, bishops, and other ministerial leaders caught in the web of homosexuality and child molestation. The sins of

31

priests and fathers, violating their young boys and men, do not just register with the Catholic church as we have seen in recent years, but also in the Protestant church and the Pentecostal church—our church. Herndon L. Davis in his magazine article, "God, Gays, and the Black Church" wrote:

> But what if the "sinner" is the pastor himself or the soloist at the early-morning service? Do the rules against homosexuality somehow change? To date, black church history has shown us that if the rules don't change, then at best they're severely bent when it comes to gay and lesbian clergy or gospel singers. From the legendary gospel great James Cleveland to the flamboyant rock and roller and gospel crooner Little Richard (and onward to some of today's most successful and respected gospel artists, ministers, and pastors), there have always been whispers, rumors, and innuendo concerning alleged private bisexual and homosexual lifestyles of some publicly anointed black church favorites. Yet there is stunning, if not astonishing, silence around them and a deep resistance to openly reprimanding high profile church figures for their "homosexual sins," despite vast common knowledge about their sexuality. According to N'Gai, although there is speculation about "...several well-known gospel music artists and ministers, I don't think any of them are willing to be truthful about who they are with other than their circle. To not be secretive could cost some of them their positions and compromise their livelihoods."[2]

A word of warning to the popular bishops and pastors who are polluting our pulpits with sin and shame—you have given angry, bitter homosexuals a loophole that fuels their stand concerning church leaders on the down low. These bishops, many of whom can be found amongst these "colleges of bishops," are actively involved in homosexuality. I have heard the sadness of bishops and pastors making their rendezvous with sin and compromise, many times right after worship services. I have had young men confess to me their many and ongoing approaches by these so-called spiritual leaders. In fact, many of these eye-witnesses and former "call boys" have, with credible resources and reference, gone on to name many of these perpetrators.

The next time you see a major "men's" conference on television, take a close look at the men on the stage. Look at the daintiness of the majority of these men who hide behind custom suits and alligator shoes. Look at their too-comfortable gestures, body language, shouts, and dances that are very similar to a woman's. Watch closely how they respond to the host pastor with unhindered attentiveness. How long can we continue to ignore the elephant in the room? Watch them closely and listen to their coded talk. The psychological lingo of a wounded man needing another man. Listen to the tones of down-low suggestions and wandering. Often at these national conferences, the "by invitation only" receptions after service are only an introductory session that can lead to sin. These down-low bishops have traveled to other countries in the name of foreign missions trips to have their sin adventures, only to have the locals calling back to America with full details of their embarrassing conduct. If the covers of mercy over the leaders of the black church were ever to be removed, it would be total calamity and collapse. Lawsuit-seeking young men would come out of the woodwork from all over the country recounting the decades of abuse and mistrust.

Our country is going to hell in a handbasket because of the demise of many church leaders across many denominational lines. Just recently in the *Charlotte Observer*, the United Church of Christ (UCC) became the largest church and Christian denomination in the United States to endorse gay marriage.[3] Nearly 80 percent of the UCC General Synod approved the resolution backing gay marriage. As if that was not bad enough, the Synod went on to encourage member churches around the country to support legislation granting equal marriage rights to gay and lesbian couples and to work against laws banning gay marriage. An opposing church leader sadly confessed, "If we had put it to a vote of the people in the pews, it would have failed overwhelmingly. This is truly Independence Day for the UCC—we have declared ourselves independent from the teaching of Scripture."

The spirit of homosexuality knows no one particular movement. The Episcopal Church consecrated an openly gay bishop in 2003. The United Methodist Church is considering reinstating an openly gay minister. The Presbyterian Church (USA) is also challenged by their policies regarding homosexual relationships.

If the church is going to lead African-American men away from the deception and disease of down-low homosexuality, it will have to be led by strong, masculine men who have the confidence, conviction, and courage of Jesus to confront sin. Mighty men of God like my spiritual father and pastor, Apostle Otis Lockett, the most integrity-filled man I have ever met in my entire life. Men like the nation's foremost apostolic apologist, Pastor Patrick L. Wooden, who was the first to see this disease among the men of the homosexual agenda, and even yours truly, Pastor Michael A. Stevens.

Not only must the man in the pulpit change, but so should the pulpit in the man change. The way in which the message is preached must change. I often observe in the black church what I call the "culture of the black church."

Why has the black church become anathema to its men today? Why has this major disconnect with its men occurred? In a recent article in the *Washington Post* entitled "No Place for Me," reporter John Fountain identified several excuses why the minister of a Pentecostal church had become disconnected from his church. When his daughter asked his wife if "Daddy [was] going to church" he began reciting his list of reasons why he would not be attending church that Sunday and probably not the following Sunday, either.

The article captured my attention for a few reasons. First, it reminds me of a time in my childhood when I asked the same question regarding our "should-have-been-the-whole-family"

34

weekly visits to church. Thank God, my father committed his life to the Lord early in my pre-teen years. Secondly, as a black man who leads other black men, I know the importance of black men being in a position to lead their families and communities as men of God. We often hear that it takes a village to raise a child, but I am convinced that it takes a church to raise a village. Finally, with the prevalent social and spiritual ills among our black men, one should see more clearly the spiritual warfare needed to counter this epidemic.

Why is there a shortage of men in today's black church? Why are our choirs allowed to dress in long robes and our men are allowed to carry on like the women in the choirs? Why is our church décor often lavender, purple, and other soft colors? What does this do for the adventurous man? Why do we have one man to every eight woman in the black church while the Nation of Islam has one woman to every eight men in their mosque? I will tell you why in two, crystal-clear words: feminine gospel. The black church experience, throughout its history, can be characterized by the preacher in his robe, screaming and sweating while delivering his sermon. My concern is that these inspirational messages cater more to the emotional side, which appeals more to women. While these sermons leave the women emotionally charged, many times they do nothing for the logical, analytical man, leaving him bored and ready for kickoff of the one o'clock football games.

The black-church culture must change. Romans 10:14 declares, "How shall they hear without a preacher?" As heralds of good news and glad tidings, it is our responsibility to preach a message that sometimes can be unpopular. God will hold us accountable for our giving in to the crowd's demands with itching ears.

> Cry aloud, spare not; lift up your voice like a trumpet; tell My people their transgression, and the house of Jacob their sins.
>
> —Isaiah 58:1

Pastors and church leaders cannot give in to homosexuals' demand that they stop preaching against the sin of homosexuality. The church cannot afford to be named among the culprits passing out condoms to protect against the consequences of sexual irresponsibility. Pastor Frank Reid is quoted in a recent article saying, "It is a serious mistake for some African-American intellectuals, gay rights activists, and liberal politicians to brand the black church as Victorian and homophobic because we lift up a different standard on the issue of sexuality. To deny a church its right to define the issues of sexual immorality, sexual preference, and safe sex for its members in a way that is consistent with the congregation's understanding of Scripture, is a form of spiritual fascism that must not be tolerated."[4]

As with most liberal, biblically-ignorant people, J. L. King's view of the black preacher is one of exaggerated judging. This too is a scheme of the devil, getting people to side with those who think all preachers wrongly condemn. We preach the real Word of God and follow Jesus' example when dealing with sin.

Once again the church is the hope of the world. I agree with King that the church could be, and should be, more involved with AIDS patients. However, I disagree with the opinion of the effectiveness, power, and presence the black church has had in the community. As a staunch defender of the black church, I am convinced it has delivered a message against sin for every AIDS victim that has slipped through the cracks of the black church. There are countless people who were reached and preached to, delivered from sin, and saved, sanctified, and set apart. Only heaven knows the number of souls that could have been AIDS victims had it not been for the black church. However, those leading a sin lifestyle that significantly contributes to the majority of new AIDS cases cannot champion this campaign. It is like expecting the tobacco industry to lead the campaign to quick smoking.

The mission of the church must change to bring wholeness

and holiness to the men who are being reclaimed from the down-low lifestyle. The culture of the church needs to change. In the culture of the typical black church today, men are not challenged to have a face-to-face encounter with God. We have "church" on Sundays. We sing, laugh, cry, and give praise, yet there is no specific period when a man can spend quality time before God to receive transformation and deliverance. The closest thing in times past was what we called "shut-ins." These were the dedicated weekends when the older saints would toil and tarry with the younger, new believers. These times were characterized by the laying on of hands, all-night prayer, fasting, casting out of demons, and baptisms of the Holy Spirit with evidence. It is sad to say, but these churches today are few. Where are the exclusive, non-distractive opportunities in which proven, mature leaders can discern, pray, and minister the Word of God with power and demonstration to the hurting souls of the men attending? "The effective, fervent prayer of a righteous man avails much" (James 5:16). Men desiring to be delivered and set free today need an encounter with God. Like Jacob of old, there must be a time when we confront the issues within our lives:

> And he arose that night and took his two wives, his two female servants, and his eleven sons, and crossed over the ford of Jabbok. He took them, sent them over the brook, and sent over what he had. Then Jacob was left alone; and a Man wrestled with him until the breaking of day. Now when He saw that He did not prevail against him, He touched the socket of his hip; and the socket of Jacob's hip was out of joint as He wrestled with him. And He said, "Let Me go, for the day breaks." But he said, "I will not let You go unless You bless me!" So He said to him, "What is your name?" And he said, "Jacob." And He said, "Your name shall no longer be called Jacob, but Israel; for you have struggled with God and with men, and have prevailed." Then Jacob asked, saying, "Tell me

Your name, I pray." And He said, "Why is it that you ask about My name?" And He blessed him there. And Jacob called the name of the place Peniel: "For I have seen God face to face, and my life is preserved."

—Genesis 32:22–30

Jacob realized at Jabbok, after he wrestled with an angel, that God not only wanted to change his name, but also his life. It was at this time that the "supplanter" or "trickster" had an encounter with God and his life was preserved.

Our church offers "encounter" retreats for men, women, or youth several times a year. These three-day retreats are held in isolated areas throughout the region, and are heavily consecrated by spiritual leaders weeks in advance. At these retreats, there is an approximate ratio of one spiritual guide/mentor for every six attendees. There are no titles, positions, or officers for those attending, therefore there is no pride or ego. There is also no room for outside distractions—no cell phones, PDA's, pagers, TV, or radio. Because of the prayer and fasting commitments by the leaders and guides weeks before the retreat, the weekends themselves provide an atmosphere of openness and transparency. There is also a very strong presence of the Lord and door-opening for deliverance and breakthrough. Demons are cast out, hearts are healed, and souls are liberated. Men who die to self (pride, arrogance, ego, rage, past sins) are able to be true men with the realizing of a divine revelation of the cross. Generational curses are exposed, freeing many men to overcome the failures and frailties of their past. True impartation and prophetic anointing occurs at the end of our retreats. Men are encouraged to join an accountability small group to continue the healing and wholeness, and for bonding and spiritual development.

CHAPTER 6

A little something for the "sistas"

To the many beautiful black women of my era, I salute you with the prophetic voice of hope and healing from the bosom of the Lordship of Jesus Christ. My heart longs for the day of your walk down the aisle of blessed matrimony, but more importantly that other walk—the walk with many fond memories of you and your husband's decades of salvation, success, and significance together. As you stroll into the sunset of God's fulfilled plan, may your life be one of faithfulness and fruitfulness. For every confused mother or wife, and every impatient single, I speak forth wholeness and wellness of mind, body, and spirit. There is hope and help is on the way.

As I observe today's Web sites concerning relationships between men and women, I find much commentary from angry, disappointed, confused, and frustrated women. Looking at the current down-low epidemic, I can imagine why. According to research conducted by Keith Boykins, the Census Bureau reported that there are more than 5 million single, black women who have never been married. There are also 3.8 million black men who are either not married, homosexuals, or incarcerated.[1] There is also this problem—if every black man took a bride, it would still leave 1.2 million black women single, by my rough figuring. This is not good—but there is hope! As my wife and I share with the single and single-again women of our church, there must be a recalling to holy living.

Abstinence for the single woman is paramount. Live patiently with faith until the Lord comes again. Live life large— go on a cruise, build a business, invest in real estate. Beware of the "dating and marriage vacuum" found in most churches. Somewhere back in time, it was assumed that if a single woman was not married by a certain age, something was wrong with her. It was always a given that women without husbands were incomplete or lacking. Oh, how wrong that was! We the church have pushed many women, and men, down the aisle of marriage without proper preparation and planning. We told them all they needed was the Holy Spirit. We somehow never told them that they also needed friendship, camaraderie, companionship, and commonality. So, to our single sisters: when preparing yourself for marital availability, seek more than just looks, money, and even the "anointing." As much as I believe that a man needs to be a proven man of God, I am convinced that women often overlook integrity, character, and honesty in their potential mates. I realize that these attributes are often intangible, so here is my "Top 10 Checklist" of things you ought to consider before you say "I do":

- Salvation check: Is he really saved? Bible-saved or self-saved?

- Church submission check: Is he an active member? What does his pastor think about him?

- Stewardship check: Does he pay his tithes and offerings? If he will steal from God, you know he will steal from you!

- Clinical health check: Does he have a clean bill of health?

- Does he have a vision for his life, and his life with you?

- Credit report check: Sis', you have worked too hard to lose it all!

- The "Does he love his momma and sisters?" check.
- The "Will he confuse you with his momma?" check.

For the dating or engaged sister, remember that God created man and man was alone. Man's problem in the Garden of Eden, as it is today, is that he really and truthfully does not want to be alone. His natural, God-given desire is for a woman, not a man. Though it sounds so "old-school," Scripture reminds us that man was not made for the woman but the woman for the man. (See 1 Corinthians 11:9). Therefore, it brings much honor to a man to find and pursue his mate into holy matrimony. Remember, he is a hunter and outdoorsman by nature; he places his eyes on the prize, pursues his target, and conquers his catch. Absolutely nothing gave me more excitement and adrenaline then courting my wife in college, casting the vision of what God was going to do in our future relationship, and then seeing it come to pass as she fully trusted in my vision and God's.

You are your husband's glory, his trophy. I believe men are attracted more to what they see than anything else; whereas, women are attracted more to what they hear than anything else. Ever wondered why you often see a beautiful lady with an ugly man? It was how he looked at the end of the day—it's what he said to her that won her. Ladies, it has always been and still is today to your advantage to look your best at all times. If for no one else, look your best for yourself. You deserve it!

For the newlywed bride, men are also recreational champions. They are truly hunters at heart. More important than being submitted, the wife has been called to be adaptable, accessible, and enjoyable. So many times we preach to our women to be submitted, submitted, and submitted. I have recently come to the conclusion that a woman can be submitted to her husband out of conviction and loyalty to God and His Word. Her submission, which is an act of her mind, does not necessarily suffice for the adaptability and accessibility that are acts of her heart and which her husband truly desires. When a man feels that his wife is only fulfilling her godly convictions by submitting without the heart and desire to please him through being adaptable and accessible, he quickly realizes that she is "duty bound" to serve and please him without shared desire. Only when the wife becomes adaptable and accessible for her husband will he feel like the champion or the hunter that he was created to be.

Take a closer look at Samson and Delilah. This woman (whom women love to hate today) actually gained the key to Sampson's heart. Women must create a haven of confidence, trust, and freedom of expression without judgment. Most men love to talk, express themselves, or communicate with passion. This is why men have no problem freely expressing themselves with each other. There is a nonjudgmental environment among men that warrants expression and acceptance. For the man who knows his purpose and loves his wife, there is no greater place than her consoling and confidence. Once that trust is tampered with by judgmental "slaps on the wrists," the man will learn to subconsciously shut down and avoid conflict. Sisters, stay encouraged! Be not dismayed; do not get weary in well doing, for the Lord is not slack concerning His promises. He is not forgetful of your labors of love. He will do everything that He said He would do—for His words will not return void. (See Isaiah 55).

Conclusion

As God spoke to Gideon—that young, fragile man who had to face his daddy's demons and destroy their altars in Judges 6—I too speak with authority to the mighty men of God who are yet to be manifested from lack of self-worth, esteem, and value. Be courageous! The whole earth today yearns and longs with great expectation for your revealing as true sons of God. Though we read and hear the Scripture time and time again, please allow 1 John 4:4 to minister to your souls, "You are of God, little children, and have overcome them, because He who is in you is greater than he who is in the world." You must now climb the walls of condemnation and confusion to victoriously hurdle over and into the God-given life He has ordained for you before the beginning of time. The church has recognized her error of avoidance and insensitivity, yet now beckons to be the bridge to wholeness and healing. The church must take her rightful place in this great and graceful equation of standard and security. The church now celebrates and commends your recovery. My prayer this day is that you would:

> *...overcome the fears of your past and even present; place your heart and your trust in the all-saving and sanctifying hand of God. Receive today the courage, conviction, and confidence to walk out the total fulfillment of man, God's man whom you have been created to be. Can these dead bones live? Yes, oh yes, man of God, they can. Allow the Father to breathe into your deflated hopes and dreams and patiently watch His miraculous doings. Ask God to give you the necessary disciplines to overcome any and all temptations that have wounded you. Finally, cry out with brokenness this day that the Lord would complete*

43

the healing process, that He who has begun a good work in you will complete it until the day of Jesus Christ. (See Philippians 1:6.) Now to Him who is able to keep you from stumbling and present you faultless with exceeding joy, to God our Savior, who alone is wise, be glory and majesty, dominion and power, both now and forever. Amen. (See Jude 24.)

Notes

INTRODUCTION

1. J.L. King, *On the Down Low: A Journey Into the Lives of "Straight" Black Men Who Sleep With Men* (New York: Harlem Moon, 2005).

2. Bill Hybels, *Courageous Leadership* (Grand Rapids, MI: Zondervan Corp., 2002), 27.

3. Margaret Downing, "Brentwood's Protests Have Given Way to a Calmer Acceptance of AIDS Patients Living There," *Houston Press*, Dec. 30, 1999.

4. Web site: www.click2houston.com, (accessed March 1, 2006).

5. J.L. King, *Coming Up From the Down Low: The Journey to Acceptance, Healing, and Honest Love*, (New York: Three Rivers Press, 2006), p. 23.

CHAPTER 1
SERIOUSNESS OF THE HOUR

1. Philip Matier, and Andrew Ross, "Epilogue for 'Stella' Author: A Messy Divorce," *San Francisco Chronicle*, June 26, 2005.

2. Ibid.

3. J.L. King, *Coming Up From the Down Low: The Journey to Acceptance, Healing, and Honest Love*, pp. 26–27.

4. Ibid., 14–15.

5. Web site: www.narth.com/docs/alleging.html, (accessed July 11, 2005).

6. Ibid.

7. Web site: www.cdc.gov/mmwr/Preview/mmwrhtm/ mm50205a2.html, "HIV/STD Rises In Young Men Who Have Sex With Men Who Do Not Disclose Their Sexual Orientation—Six U.S. Cities, 1994–2000," (accessed Feb. 7, 2003).

8. Gregory A. Freeman, "Bug Chasers: The Men Who Long to be HIV-Positive," *Rolling Stone*, Feb. 6, 2003.

9. Randall Robinson, *Quitting America* (New York: Dutton Adult, 2004), 19–21.

10. Ibid.

11. Dr. Jawanza Kunjufu, *Countering the Conspiracy to Destroy Black Boys* (Chicago, IL: African American Images, 1985).

12. Web site: http://www.med.umich.edu/1libr/aha/umafamer04 .htm (accessed May 1, 2006).

13. Web site: http://www.batonrougeaidssociety.com/_wsn/page13 .html (accessed May 1, 2006).

CHAPTER 2

Homosexuals in Denial

1. Web site: www.cdc.gov/mmwr/Preview/mmwrhtm/ mm50205a2.html, "HIV/STD Rises In Young Men Who Have Sex With Men Who Do Not Disclose Their Sexual Orientation—Six U.S. Cities, 1994–2000," (accessed Feb. 7, 2003).

2. J.L. King, *On the Down Low: A Journey Into the Lives of "Straight" Black Men Who Sleep With Men*, 147–152.

3. Ibid., 34.

4. Neale Donald Walsch, *Conversations With God* (New York: Putnam Adult, 1996).

5. J.L. King, *On the Down Low: A Journey Into the Lives of "Straight" Black Men Who Sleep With Men*, 17–23.

6. Ibid., iv.

7. Web site: www.narth.com/docs/istheregene.html, (accessed Sept. 21, 2004).

8. The American Psychological Association, *Answers to Your Questions About Sexual Orientation and Homosexuality* (pamphlet, 2004).

9. Simon LeVay, *Queer Science* (Cambridge, MA: MIT Press, 1996).

10. Steven Goldberg, *When Wish Replaces Thought: Why So Much of What You Believe Is False* (Buffalo, NY: Prometheus Books, 1994).

11. Web site: www.narth.com/docs/istheregene.html (accessed Sept. 21, 2004).

12. Web site: www.narth.com/docs/drphil2.html, "Dr. Phil Gets It Wrong About Homosexual Behavior," (accessed Nov. 3, 2005).

CHAPTER 3

Advice From the Down Low Is Useless

1. J.L. King, *On the Down Low: A Journey Into the Lives of "Straight" Black Men Who Sleep With Men*, 25.

2. Ibid., 166.

3. Keith Boykins, *Beyond the Down Low: Sex, Lies, and Denial in Black America* (New York: Carroll & Graf, 2005), 255.

4. Ibid., 214.

5. Ibid., 219.

6. Web site: www.pastors.com, "Pastors Must Reclaim Counselor's Role on Homosexuality" by Erin Curry, (accessed Apr. 21, 2006).

7. Ibid.

8. Web site: www.narth.com/docs/pastor.html, "Ex-Gay Now Baptist Pastor Speaks to Campus Group," (accessed Oct. 14, 2005).

9. J.L. King, *On the Down Low: A Journey Into the Lives of "Straight" Black Men Who Sleep With Men*, xiv.

10. J.L. King, *Coming Up From the Down Low*, 185.

CHAPTER 4
ENCOURAGE, EQUIP, AND EDIFY

1. Web site: www.peoplecanchange.com/Is_Change_Possible.htm, (accessed Mar. 1, 2005).

2. Web site: www.saintaugustinechurch.org/university/wisdom/happiness.html, (accessed Apr. 21, 2006).

CHAPTER 5
WHAT THE CHURCH MUST DO RIGHT NOW

1. Brian Keith Williams, *Ministering Graciously to the Gay and Lesbian Community: Learning to Relate and Understand* (Shippensburg, PA: Destiny Image Publishers, 2005).

2. Herndon L. Davis, "God, Gays, and the Black Church: Keeping the Faith Within the Black Community," (special to AOL's e-zine) *Black Voices*, www.aol.com, (accessed: Sept. 1, 2005).

3. John Fountain, "No Place For Me," *Washington Post*, July 17, 2005.

CHAPTER 6
A LITTLE SOMETHING FOR THE "SISTAS"

1. Keith Boykins, *Beyond the Down Low: Sex, Lies, and Denial in Black America*.